The Tiger Rising

by Kate DiCamillo

Lit Link
Grades 4-6

Written by Nat Reed
Illustrated by S&S Learning Materials

About the author:
Nat Reed has been a member of the teaching profession for over 30 years.
He is presently a full-time instructor at Trent University in the Teacher Education Program.

ISBN: 978-1-55495-000-3
Copyright 2009

All Rights Reserved * Printed in Canada

Published in the U.S.A by:
On The Mark Press
P.O. Box 433
Clayton, New York
13624
www.onthemarkpress.com

Published in Canada by:
S&S Learning Materials
15 Dairy Avenue
Napanee, Ontario
K7R 1M4
www.sslearning.com

At A Glance

Learning Expectations	Chapters 1-2	Chapters 3-4	Chapters 5-6	Chapters 7-8	Chapters 9-10	Chapters 11-12	Chapters 13-14	Chapters 15-16	Chapters 17-18	Chapters 19-20	Chapters 21-22	Chapters 23-24	Chapters 25-26	Chapters 27-28	Chapters 29-30
Reading Comprehension															
• Identify and describe story elements	•	•		•	•		•	•	•	•	•	•	•	•	•
• Summarize events/details	•	•	•	•	•	•	•	•	•	•	•	•	•	•	•
Reasoning & Critical Thinking Skills															
• Character traits, comparisons	•	•		•	•	•	•	•	•		•	•	•	•	•
• Use context clues	•	•	•	•	•	•	•		•	•	•	•		•	•
• Make inferences (why events occurred, characters' thoughts and feelings)	•	•	•	•	•	•	•	•	•	•	•	•	•	•	•
• Determine the meaning of colloquialisms and other phrases						•					•	•			
• Understand abstract concepts – conscience, revenge, fear, perseverance, self-respect, exaggeration, conflict, etc.	•	•						•			•	•	•	•	•
• Develop opinions and personal interpretations	•	•	•	•	•	•	•		•	•	•	•	•	•	•
• Write a letter/newspaper editorial									•						
• Conduct an interview											•				
• Identify/create a *simile*	•														
• Identify *alliteration*		•													
• Identify *onomatopoeia*													•		
• Identify *foreshadowing*														•	
• Identify an *analogy*											•				
• Identify *personification*			•				•								
• Identify an *idiom*											•				
• Identify *conflict*												•			
• Identify the *climax* of a story															•
• Complete a synopsis											•	•			
• Complete a poster/book cover												•		•	
• Complete a Story Map															•
• Create a storyboard													•		
• Create a poem	•								•						
• Create a reader's theatre presentation												•			
• Practice research skills		•		•	•	•	•			•	•				
• Create an Observation Chart										•					
• Predict an outcome						•					•			•	•
Vocabulary Development, Grammar, & Word Usage															
• Identify synonyms, antonyms, and homonyms		•	•	•	•					•	•		•	•	•
• Identify syllables		•													
• Identify compound words														•	
• Identify parts of speech											•	•			
• Dictionary and thesaurus skills	•	•	•	•	•	•		•	•	•	•	•	•	•	•
• Place words in alphabetical order						•									
• Identify singular/plural				•											
• Identify root words											•				
• Using capitals, correct punctuation						•									

The Tiger Rising
By Kate DiCamillo

Table of Contents

The Tiger Rising
By Kate DiCamillo

Overall Expectations

The students will:

- develop their skills in reading, writing, listening, and oral communication.

- use good literature as a vehicle for developing skills required by curriculum expectations: reasoning and critical thinking, knowledge of language structure, vocabulary building, and use of conventions.

- become meaningfully engaged in the drama of literature through a variety of types of questions and activities.

- identify and describe elements of stories (i.e. plot, main idea, characters, setting).

- learn and review many skills in order to develop good reading habits.

- provide clear answers to questions and well-constructed explanations.

- organize and classify information to clarify thinking.

- learn about the dynamics of grief, anger, and isolation, coping with the loss of a parent, forging healthy relationships, accepting responsibility for one's actions.

- learn the healthiness of expressing one's feelings/needs to those close to us.

- relate events and feelings found in the novel to the student's own lives and experiences.

- appreciate the importance of friends and how relationships can contribute to personal growth.

- appreciate that the growth of one's character is often the result of opportunities and trials that come into one's life.

- learn the importance of dealing with adversity and developing perseverance in the face of difficult experiences.

- state their own interpretation of a written work, using evidence from the novel and from their own knowledge and experience.

The Tiger Rising
By Kate DiCamillo

List of Skills

Vocabulary Development:
1. Using content clues
2. Locating descriptive words/phrases
3. Listing synonyms, antonyms, homonyms
4. Use of capitals and punctuation
5. Identifying syllables
6. Listing compound words
7. Determining alphabetical order
8. Use of singular/plural nouns
9. Developing dictionary skills
10. Identifying parts of speech
11. Identify an *analogy*
12. Identifying an *idiom*
13. Identifying a *simile*
14. Identifying *alliteration*
15. Identify *onomatopoeia*
16. Identify *personification*

Setting Activities:
1. Identify the details of a setting

Plot Activities:
1. Complete a *Story Map*
2. Determine the role of others in one's personal growth
3. Identify the *climax* of a novel
4. Identify *conflict* in the story
5. Develop a Storyboard
6. Identify point of view
7. Predict an outcome

Character Activities:
1. Determine character traits
2. Compare two characters
3. Relating personal experiences
4. Understand concepts: *coping with loss, friendship*

Creative and Critical Thinking:
1. Research
2. Create a Reader's Theatre presentation
3. Write a letter to a character from the novel
4. Conduct an interview
5. Create an Observation Chart
6. Write a description of personal feelings
7. Create a poem

Art Activities:
1. Design a cover for the novel
1. Develop a Storyboard
2. Design a poster

The Tiger Rising
By Kate DiCamillo

Teacher Suggestions

This resource can be used in a variety of ways:

1. The student booklet focuses on one chapter of the novel at a time. Each of these sections contains the following activities:

   a) **Before You Read The Chapters** (reasoning and critical thinking skills)
   b) **Vocabulary Building** (dictionary and thesaurus skills)
   c) **Questions on the Chapter** (reading comprehension skills)
   d) **Language Activities** (grammar, punctuation, word structure and extension activities)

2. Students may read the novel at their own speed and then select, or be assigned, a variety of questions and activities.

3. **Bulletin Board and Interest Center Ideas:** Themes might include tigers, circus animals, endangered species, mistreatment of animals, the Sistine Chapel, Michelangelo, and Florida.

4. **Pre-Reading Activities.** The Tiger Rising may also be used in conjunction with themes of loss of a parent; handling grief, anger and isolation; bullying; the importance of friendship; endangered species; tigers; psychosomatic illnesses.

5. **Independent Reading Approach:** Students who are able to work independently may attempt to complete the assignments in a self-directed manner. Initially these students should participate in the pre-reading activities with the rest of the class. Students should familiarize themselves with the reproducible student booklet. Completed worksheets should be submitted so that the teacher can note how quickly and accurately the students are working. Students may be brought together periodically to discuss issues in specific sections of the novel.

6. **Fine Art Activities:** Students may integrate such topics as tigers, endangered animals, the Sistine Chapel, and Michelangelo's artwork. Students will be given the opportunity to complete a book cover, poster and Storyboard.

7. Encourage the students to keep a reading log in which they record their readings each day and their thoughts about the passage.

8. Students should keep all their work together in one place. A portfolio cover is provided for this reason.

9. Students should not be expected to complete all activities. Teachers should allow choice and in some cases, match the activity to the student's ability.

10. Students should keep track (in their portfolio) of the activities they complete.

The Tiger Rising
By Kate DiCamillo

Synopsis

Following his mother's death, Rob Horton and his dad move from Jacksonville to Lister, Florida, where he and his dad take up residence in a seedy motel. Rob keeps all of his emotions "locked in a suitcase", refusing to share his feelings with anyone. Ugly red blisters have appeared on Rob's legs, prompting the principal of his school to send him home in case he is *contagious*. Walking through the misty Florida woods one morning, Rob is stunned to encounter a real-life tiger pacing back and forth in a cage. On the very same day, Rob also meets Sistine Bailey, a girl who shows her feelings as readily as Rob hides his. Gradually the two become friends and through the counsel of the motel maid, Willie May, and their experiences with the tiger, learn the importance of sharing their feelings with those they love, and trusting their friends with their emotions.

Author Biography
Kate DiCamillo

Born in Philadelphia, Pennsylvania in 1964, Kate and her family were forced to move to Florida when she was five years old because she suffered from chronic pneumonia. The doctors felt that the warmer climate would be good for Kate's health. Kate majored in English at the University of Florida and then when she was 30, moved to Minneapolis. While working in a book warehouse she met a representative for Candlewick Press and submitted the manuscript for **Because of Winn-Dixie** – her first of many successful novels. Three of her novels, **Because of Winn-Dixie, The Tale of Despereaux** and **The Miraculous Journey of Edward Tulane** have been made into major motion pictures. As is the case with **The Tiger Rising**, animals generally play a prominent role in her novels.

Kate currently lives in Minneapolis, Minnesota, where she faithfully writes two pages a day, five days a week.

The Tiger Rising
By Kate DiCamillo

Student Checklist

Student Name: _____

Assignment	Grade/Level	Comments

The Tiger Rising

By Kate DiCamillo

Name: _____

The Tiger Rising
By Kate DiCamillo

Chapters 1 & 2

Before you read the chapters:

Anna Julia Cooper wrote, "Bullies are always cowards at heart and may be credited with a pretty safe instinct in scenting their prey." Why do you think it is dangerous to witness someone being bullied and not do anything about it?

_____

_____

_____

Vocabulary:

Choose a word from the list to complete each sentence.

creeping	lurch	pretend	melody	concentrating
harbors	sullen	notion	astounded	abiding

1. I don't think my brother _____ any bitter feelings toward his boss.

2. Wherever did you get the _____ that you didn't need to bring your pencil?

3. My mother had the _____ belief that all things would work out.

4. Misty was simply _____ when she passed the math test.

5. It was obvious that Mickey was unhappy by the _____ look on his face.

6. The sudden movement of the ship caused him to _____ and fall into the pool.

7. "I'm sorry I didn't hear you," he said. "I was _____ on what I was reading."

8. Matilda saw a huge spider _____ across the living room floor.

9. It is said that her uncle created a _____ to go with the words of that poem.

10. It won't do any good to _____ you're sick, your homework will still have to be done for tomorrow's class.

The Tiger Rising
By Kate DiCamillo

Questions:

1. Why did Rob like the Kentucky Star sign?

   _____

   _____

2. From the second paragraph in Chapter One, how do we know that Rob definitely does not like going to school?

   _____

   _____

3. Do you think that the tiger Rob found, beside the Beauchamp gas station building, was real? Defend your answer.

   _____

   _____

4. What three things was Rob not thinking about as he waited for the bus?

   _____

   _____

5. Rob has a very rich imagination. What way has he devised for not thinking about things?

   _____

   _____

6. What is the **setting** for this novel? Remember a setting consists of both a time and place.

   _____

   _____

7. Bullying can take many forms. Two ways that Norton and Billy bullied Rob were physically and verbally. Give an example of each.

   _____

   _____

8. What surprising event took place at the end of Chapter Two?

_____

_____

Language Activities:

1. A **literary device** the author enjoys using is *a simile* (a comparison using *like* or *as*). An example of this is when the author writes, "He specifically did not think about Norton and Billy Threemonger waiting for him like chained and starving guard dogs, eager to attack." With what does the author compare Norton and Billy?

_____

Come up with three similes of your own that have a definite *tiger-like* flavor.

_____

_____

_____

2. **A Name Poem**

A Name Poem, or Acrostic Poem, tells about the topic (or name) of the poem. It uses the letters of the word for the first letter of each line. Here is an example.

> **MILK**
>
> **M**oo cows
> **I**n farmland
> **L**ike to be milked, but
> **K**ick me when my hands are cold.

• Now write a Name Poem of at least four lines.

• Possible topics: tiger, school, buses, bully.

_____

_____

_____

_____

The Tiger Rising
By Kate DiCamillo

Chapters 3 & 4

Before you read the chapters:

In these two chapters Sistine attends a new school for the first time. New experiences like this can be very stressful. Describe a time in your own life when you experienced something for the first time. Be sure to mention your feelings during this experience.

_____

_____

_____

Vocabulary:

Using words from this chapter, complete the following crossword puzzle.

CRUD	TIGER	CHASES	CONES	RAM	ROUTE	PHELMER
WANDER	BEAUCHAMP	KENTUCKY	HORTON	BILLY	BED	
ENTER	SULLEN	SISTINE	BLISTER	EYE	TALES	
MISTER	EVIL	GLARE	SNOB	DEERE	DISEASE	
BAILEY	LACY	TAG	EVERYONE	ROBERT	RIB	

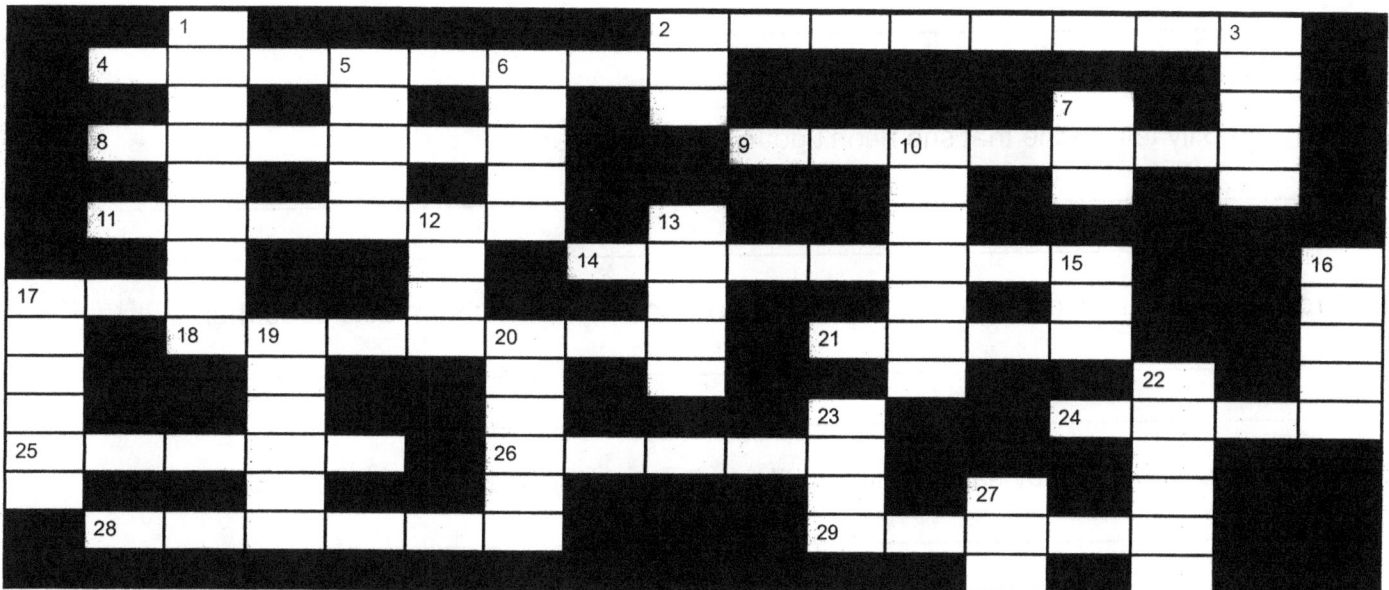

The Tiger Rising
By Kate DiCamillo

Down

1. Name of a gas station
2. An organ for sight
3. Computer keyboard key
5. Stories
6. Ice Cream _____
7. A children's game
10. The new girl's first name
12. Very bad
13. A fixed angry stare
15. Chest bone
16. One of Rob's bullies
17. _____ Horton
19. Rob's surname
20. Mr.
22. Sistine's surname
23. Rob was accused of having the creeping _____.
27. Where one often sleeps

Across

2. All people
4. The _____ Star Motel
8. Crabby or gloomy looking
9. A sickness
11. Pursues
14. Sin sore
17. A male sheep
18. The principal of Rob's school
21. A stuck-up person
24. Sistine wore a pink _____ dress.
25. A way, or road for passage or travel
26. A member of the cat family
28. To ramble aimlessly
29. Billy wore a John _____ cap.

Questions:

1. Why did Billy and Norton call Rob *disease boy*?

   _____

   _____

2. Why did Billy tell Sistine that she hadn't got on the party bus?

   _____

   _____

3. From what we know about Sistine in these two chapters, record three facts about her.

   _____

   _____

4. What does Rob mean by saying "He kept the suitcase closed" at the end of Chapter 3?

   _____

   _____

5. Where was Sistine from? What was her impression of the South?

_____

_____

6. The last paragraph of Chapter 4 gives us another clue as to how Rob is regarded by the kids in his class. What incident are we referring to?

_____

_____

Language Activities:

Alliteration

Alliteration is the repetition of the first consonant sound in a phrase. An example is: *she sells seashells by the seashore.* An example from Chapter Four: *what he wanted to do was whittle in wood.*

1. Can you find the example of alliteration in the first three paragraphs of Chapter 3?

_____

2. Create your own alliterations using the following ideas:

a) Describe the sound of two cats fighting.

_____

b) Invent your own idea here!

_____

Extension Activity:

Sistine was named after the Sistine Chapel. Using resources in your school library or the Internet, investigate this marvelous building and record three interesting facts about it.

_____

_____

_____

The Tiger Rising
By Kate DiCamillo

Chapters 5 & 6

Before you read the chapters:

Sticking up for someone else or standing up to a bully takes a lot of courage. Describe a time when you either witnessed such an event or were part of it yourself. Describe how you felt at the time.

_____

_____

_____

_____

What are some things that make kids different and stand out? How can this sometimes be a good thing?

_____

_____

_____

Vocabulary:

In each of the following sets of words, underline the one word that does not belong. Then write a sentence explaining why it does not fit.

1. interact   mingle   mesh   council

_____

2. contagious   catching   selfish   communicable

_____

3. manifest   concentrated   thought   engrossed

_____

4. buoyed   sabotaged   encouraged   inspired

_____

5. communicate   conversation   impart   possibility

_____

6. array   vestibule   multitude   variety

_____

7. fortitude   astonishing   remarkable   unbelievable

_____

Questions:

Cloze Call

Complete the following exercise filling in the correct words from the Word Box.

contagious	tiger	run	something	great	mother
kicking	looked	home	interact	legs	kids
doctor	note	worried	breezeway	never	lunchroom

Mr. Phelmer always began his talks with Rob by saying, "Rob, we're a bit _____."
The fact that Rob didn't _____ with other students was a concern. Mr. Phelmer
asked Rob if he was putting medicine on his _____. Some parents were worried
that Rob's rash might be _____. A _____ in Jacksonville gave Rob
the medicine. Mr. Phelmer suggested that Rob stay at _____ until his rash cleared
up. Rob thought that was a _____ idea. When visiting the principal, Rob felt the
picture of the _____ burning in his pocket. After his visit with Mr. Phelmer was
over, the principal gave him a _____ to take home. Rob knew that his legs would
_____ clear up.

At lunch, Rob sat on the benches in the _____. Nothing had tasted good to him
since his _____ died. Sistine Bailey then came through the _____
doors followed by a crowd of _____. When someone threw _____
at Sistine she turned and started swinging with her fists, _____ and twirling. When
Rob told the kids to leave her alone, they _____ at him. After a minute, Rob decided
to _____.

The Tiger Rising
By Kate DiCamillo

Language Activities:

1. Choose <u>ten</u> words from these chapters with two or more **syllables**. Indicate the syllables by drawing a line between each one. **Example: ti/ger.**

_____   _____

_____   _____

_____   _____

_____   _____

_____   _____

Another **literary device** the author enjoys using is **personification**. Personification is when an inanimate object (usually a non-living or non-human object such as a ship) is given human characteristics. A rather unusual example of this is in Chapter 5 when the author writes, "He concentrated on keeping his heart from singing out loud with joy." What object is personified in this sentence, and what human action is it accomplishing?

_____

_____

Think of an interesting inanimate object and create a sentence in which this object is personified.

_____

_____

_____

The Tiger Rising
By Kate DiCamillo

Chapters 7 & 8

Before you read the chapters:

It can be difficult to be a child of a single parent. Think of an example of one such difficulty and one possible benefit to such a situation or arrangement.

_____

_____

_____

_____

Vocabulary:

Draw a straight line to connect the vocabulary word to its definition. Remember to use a straight edge (like a ruler).

1.	extraordinary	a.	everlasting
2.	regret	b.	to lean or lie back
3.	permanent	c.	ease
4.	contagious	d.	imagine
5.	recline	e.	unusual
6.	desperate	f.	care or upkeep
7.	relieve	g.	focus
8.	pretend	h.	to feel remorse
9.	maintenance	i.	reckless
10.	concentrate	j.	catching

The Tiger Rising
By Kate DiCamillo

Questions:

1. What extraordinary events had Rob already experienced in the first six chapters? (Describe three of these.)

   _____

   _____

   _____

2. Why do you think it was Rob's policy "not to say things?"

   _____

   _____

3. Rob's dad tells him that they are staying at the motel only until "they can get back on their feet." What does this expression mean?

   _____

   _____

4. Why do you think Rob's father decided to give Rob a few days off school?

   _____

   _____

5. What do you think of the advice Rob's dad gives him about fighting back against the boys at school?

   _____

   _____

6. Why do you think Rob was relieved when he couldn't go outside to see the tiger because it was raining too hard?

   _____

   _____

7. Why do you think Rob ended up carving Sistine instead of the tiger?

   _____

   _____

The Tiger Rising
By Kate DiCamillo

Language Activities:

Write the plural of the following nouns from this chapter. Be careful – you may wish to consult a dictionary for some of these words.

Singular Noun	Plural Noun
body	
man	
roof	
person	
macaroni	
dress	
ointment	
foot	

Extension Activity:

Frescoes

In Chapter 7, Rob mentions that the paintings on the ceiling of the Sistine Chapel were **frescoes**. Using resources in your school library or on the Internet, investigate frescoes and briefly describe this artistic technique.

_____

_____

_____

_____

_____

_____

The Tiger Rising
By Kate DiCamillo

Chapters 9 & 10

Before you read the chapters:

In this section, Willie May, the housekeeper, encourages Rob to return to school. Can you predict what the main reason Willie May offers Rob for continuing his education? (After you read these two chapters, come back and see how close you were to the actual reason Willie May gives.)

_____

_____

_____

_____

Vocabulary:

Choose a word from the list that means the same (synonym) or nearly the same as the underlined word.

capable	licorice	desperate	certificates
personal	rhythm	extended	adjust

1. My aunt considered her age to be a **private** matter.

2. He **lengthened** the shelf by quite a bit.

3. When the baby went missing, the mother became **frantic**.

4. It was difficult for Miss Thompson to **adapt** to the climate change.

5. The boy was given a piece of **candy** to keep him occupied.

6. A finished carpenter is **able** to build any piece of furniture.

7. Several framed **documents** lined the principal's walls.

8. The audience found the **beat** of the song very appealing.

The Tiger Rising
By Kate DiCamillo

Questions:

1. Why didn't Rob ever make a wish on his own personal shooting star?

   _____

   _____

2. Give an example of exaggeration from the first half of Chapter 9.

   _____

   _____

3. Rob's hair was described as "cobwebby blond." What do you think was meant by the adjective "cobwebby" in this description?

   _____

   _____

4. Why did Rob's dad stop singing halfway through the song "Mining for Gold?"

   _____

   _____

5. What famous baseball player had a name very similar to the housekeeper in Chapter 10, Willie May?

   _____

6. What incentive did Willie May offer Rob for staying in school?

   _____

   _____

7. What did Willie May suggest was the reason for the problem with the rash on Rob's legs? Do you agree?

   _____

   _____

   _____

The Tiger Rising
By Kate DiCamillo

Language Activities:

Place the following words from these chapters in **alphabetical order**.

star		1	
stop		2	
suitcase		3	
stared		4	
squeak		5	
swamp		6	
shyly		7	
smashing		8	
steam		9	
softly		10	

Extension Activity:

Mining For Gold

The song, *Mining for Gold*, was a popular recording by the **Cowboy Junkies**. The lyrics eloquently speak of the hardships hard rock miners have endured over the years. Find a copy of the lyrics to this song on the Internet and write a brief synopsis of the three verses.

Why do you think this song appealed to Rob's dad at this time?

_____

_____

_____

_____

The Tiger Rising
By Kate DiCamillo

Chapters 11 & 12

Before you read the chapters:

Making new friends can be a risky business. What might be one pitfall in developing a friendship with another person?

_____

_____

_____

_____

Vocabulary:

Solve the following word search puzzle using the words from the **Word Box**. Remember – the words can be horizontal, vertical or diagonal. They may be forward or even backward!

SISTINE	CHEEKBONES	KENTUCKY	CEMENT	CONCENTRATED
LEPROSY	ACCURATE	RECOGNIZE	EQUATION	DROOPY
MACARONI	MICHELANGELO	SCULPTOR	ARC	DEFIANT

C	P	O	D	E	T	A	R	T	N	E	C	N	O	C
H	M	A	C	A	R	O	N	I	I	U	Y	T	E	E
E	R	I	A	C	C	U	R	A	T	E	A	M	K	D
E	G	E	C	N	O	I	T	A	U	Q	E	Q	E	C
K	H	P	C	H	N	J	D	D	F	N	S	W	N	V
B	J	O	Q	O	E	S	I	S	T	I	N	E	T	B
O	Y	I	W	X	G	L	F	S	D	Z	D	W	U	T
N	K	S	E	C	B	N	A	R	C	X	F	E	C	N
E	L	U	O	V	V	K	I	N	F	C	G	R	K	A
S	H	Y	R	R	C	L	G	Z	G	V	H	T	Y	I
D	S	C	U	L	P	T	O	R	E	E	J	Y	V	F
F	G	T	T	B	X	E	H	G	H	B	L	U	C	E
D	F	R	Y	N	Z	M	L	B	Y	P	O	O	R	D

The Tiger Rising
By Kate DiCamillo

Questions:

1. What disease did Norton suggest Rob had?

   _____

   _____

2. Why do you think when Rob was speaking with Sistine he was so determined to *keep his words inside himself, where they belonged?*

   _____

   _____

3. Why do you think something inside Rob opened up when he saw Sistine's small pinched face, bleeding knuckles and dark eyes?

   _____

   _____

   _____

4. Describe Sistine's reaction to seeing Rob's sculptures for the first time.

   _____

   _____

5. What does the fact that when Rob is embarrassed, he has to calm down the rash on his legs, suggest about his illness?

   _____

   _____

6. Why do you think Rob would never wish for a friend?

   _____

   _____

The Tiger Rising
By Kate DiCamillo

Language Activities:

Rewrite the following sentences putting in the **correct capitalization** and **punctuation**.

rob and sistine lived in the town of lister

_____

_____

why do you think principal phelmer was worried about rob

_____

_____

this august we will be visiting boston pittsburgh and toronto on our vacation

_____

_____

Extension Activity:

Michelangelo

Michelangelo was an Italian Renaissance painter, sculptor, architect, poet and engineer. He lived from 1475-1564 and during this time, probably accomplished more than any artist who ever lived. Using resources in your school library or on the Internet, research more of the life and accomplishments of this interesting man. Record three facts below that you uncovered which you consider especially noteworthy.

_____

_____

_____

_____

_____

The Tiger Rising
By Kate DiCamillo

Chapters 13 & 14

Before you read the chapters:

Rob seems to be a boy who hasn't had much happiness in his life lately. What things make you happy? Try to think of at least three things.

_____

_____

_____

_____

Vocabulary:

Write a **sentence** using the following words. Make sure that the meaning of the word is clear in your sentence.

culture: _____

_____

whittle: _____

_____

protest: _____

_____

trespass: _____

_____

The Tiger Rising
By Kate DiCamillo

gesture: _____

_____

wary: _____

_____

enormous: _____

_____

exertion: _____

_____

Questions:

1. Describe how Sistine ended up living in Lister, Florida.

_____

_____

2. Find an example of **personification** in the first three paragraphs of Chapter 13.

_____

_____

3. a) Why was Rob so reluctant to tell Sistine that his mother had died?

_____

_____

b) Why was Sistine so upset that Rob wouldn't talk about his mother to her?

_____

_____

The Tiger Rising
By Kate DiCamillo

4. Why did Rob find it so hard to look at the tiger?

_____

_____

5. What did Sistine suggest they do with the tiger?

_____

_____

6. How did Rob describe his feeling of happiness?

_____

_____

Extension Activity:

William Blake

William Blake was an English poet who lived from 1757 to 1827. Although he was largely unappreciated during his lifetime, his poems are now considered tremendously important in English literature. One of his most famous poems was one entitled "The Tiger," which Sistine refers to in Chapter 14 and later in Chapter 29. In your school library or on the Internet, investigate the poems of this gifted writer. Record a verse below from one of his poems that you found very appealing. Below the verse, explain why you enjoyed it.

_____

_____

_____

_____

_____

_____

_____

_____

The Tiger Rising
By Kate DiCamillo

Chapters 15 & 16

Before you read the chapters:

Sistine is having trouble adjusting to life in Lister. What would be difficult about moving to a new town? (If you have ever moved to a new place, you might wish to relate your own experiences in answering this question.)

_____

_____

_____

_____

Vocabulary:

Choose a word from the list to complete each definition.

evaporate	stalk	forbidden	congressman	concentrate
constellation	squint	grease	disbelief	profile

1. To look with one's eyes partly closed is to _____.

2. A formation of stars is known as a _____.

3. _____ is the process of liquid turning to vapor.

4. _____ is a type of lubricant.

5. To think really hard is to _____.

6. To pursue stealthily is to _____.

7. A _____ is a politician.

8. If you are _____ to do something, you will probably get into trouble if you disobey.

9. _____ means that you are having trouble buying someone's story.

10. A side view of an object is known as a _____.

The Tiger Rising
By Kate DiCamillo

Questions:

1. When Rob's father asks Sistine if she lives around there, Sistine replies, "For now." What does this tell you about Sistine's attitude?

_____

_____

2. How do we know that Sistine was put out about using the phone in the laundry room?

_____

_____

3. Re-read the concluding paragraph in Chapter 15. What does the author mean by the statement "He shook his head and scolded himself for opening his suitcase?"

_____

_____

_____

4. Describe how Sistine's parents met?

_____

_____

5. Why did Rob and his dad move to Lister from Jacksonville?

_____

_____

6. a) Briefly describe your impression of Sistine's mother.

_____

_____

b) Why do you think that she and Sistine do not get along?

_____

_____

The Tiger Rising
By Kate DiCamillo

Extension Activity:

Write a **synopsis** of the events of Chapters 15-16.

_____

_____

_____

_____

_____

_____

_____

_____

Your Choice

Choose **one** of the following activities:

- With two or three other students create a Readers' Theatre presentation to be performed in front of the class <u>or</u> act out a scene from the novel.

- Find a song or a poem that reminds you of a scene or character from <u>The Tiger Rising</u>.
  Write out the song or poem on a separate sheet of paper.

- Write a detailed description of either Rob, Sistine or Willie May. Draw or cut out a picture to accompany the description.

- Write a letter to one of the characters in the novel, then write the letter that he or she might send back to you <u>or</u> write a letter to Kate DiCamillo, the novel's author.

The Tiger Rising

By Kate DiCamillo

Chapters 17 & 18

Before you read the chapters:

Rob, Sistine and Willie May are all very memorable people that we have met thus far in this novel. In Chapter 18, Rob meets another colorful character – Mr. Beauchamp. Who would you say is the most unusual person you have ever met? What was there about this person that made him/her so interesting?

_____

_____

_____

_____

Vocabulary:

Synonyms are words with similar meanings. Using the context of the sentences below, choose the best synonym for the underlined words in each sentence.

1. Stella decided to ask for her brother's **opinion**.
   a) turntable   b) advice   c) purpose   d) allowance

2. I saw the parakeet **flitting** about the cage.
   a) scrambling   b) running   c) flying   d) darting

3. The foaming sea waves **billowed** out all round the little vessel.
   a) swelled   b) roared   c) calmed   d) brushed

4. The kindergarten teacher **suspended** the mobile from the ceiling before her class entered.
   a) broke   b) hung   c) dusted   d) tore

5. The boys were **draped** all over the railing.
   a) spitting   b) writing   c) hanging   d) dancing

6. A **fervent** light seemed to shine from his eyes.
   a) intense   b) dull   c) yellowish   d) angry

7. The engine required daily **maintenance** from Jackie and her dad.
   a) cleaning   b) watering   c) oiling   d) upkeep

The Tiger Rising
By Kate DiCamillo

Questions:

1. a) Why do you think Rob asked Willie May her opinion about zoos?

_____

_____

   b) Write a brief synopsis of the story Willie May told Rob about the parakeet her dad gave to her.

_____

_____

_____

_____

2. What is your impression of Mr. Beauchamp's personality? Give proof for your points.

_____

_____

_____

3. Rob is in a dilemma when Beauchamp takes him to see the tiger. He wants desperately to go to see the tiger but at the same time wishes that Willie May or his father would appear to save him from going with Beauchamp. Why do you think he has such mixed feelings?

_____

_____

_____

4. Beauchamp tells Rob that he is going to give him an opportunity to make some extra money. Predict how Rob will earn this money.

_____

_____

The Tiger Rising
By Kate DiCamillo

Language Activities:

1. Copy out any three sentences from these chapters and underline the **verbs**.

   _____

   _____

   _____

   _____

   _____

2. Beside each of the following words from these two chapters, write its **root word**.

   a) folding _____   b) nodded _____

   c) finally _____   d) going _____

3. The word **"fold"** can be used as a **noun** or a **verb**, depending on the sentence. Use your imagination and write sentences to illustrate how this word can be used as both a noun and a verb.

   Fold as a **noun.**

   _____

   _____

   _____

   _____

   Fold as a **verb.**

   _____

   _____

   _____

   _____

The Tiger Rising
By Kate DiCamillo

Observation Chart

How careful an observer are you? *The Tiger Rising* is a novel rich with sights, sounds, and smells. Review the chapters you have read thus far and collect as many examples of the five senses as you can find. These examples should be listed in the chart below. An example of smell is found in Chapter 18: "The bag was heavy and it stunk." See if you can get at least one example for each sense.

SIGHT	
SOUND	
TOUCH	
TASTE	
SMELL	

The Parakeet

Willie May tells Rob a story about when she was a little girl and had a pet **parakeet**. Parakeets do make interesting and popular pets. The most common pet parakeet is probably the **budgerigar** or **budgie**. Investigate the parakeet and record below three interesting facts about this fascinating bird.

_____

_____

_____

_____

The Tiger Rising
By Kate DiCamillo

Chapters 19 & 20

Before you read the chapters:

Investigate: Tigers are one of the world's most famous species of wild animal, yet what do you really know about this fascinating beast? List below <u>five</u> things you already know about tigers. (If you can't come up with five items, you may have to do some research in your school library or on the Internet.)

_____

_____

_____

_____

Vocabulary:

Antonyms are words with opposite meanings. Draw a line from each word in column A to its antonym in column B. Then use the words in column A to fill in the blanks in the sentences below.

Column A	Column B
insist	uneasiness
tattered	ordinary
desperate	sincere
amazing	shout
mocking	suggest
comfort	new
whisper	hopeful

1. I would appreciate if you all would _____ because my son is trying to sleep.

2. From their applause, the audience obviously thought the magician's tricks were absolutely

    _____ .

3. After working for twelve straight hours on my homework, I am in _____ need of a nap.

4. The hobo's clothes were _____ and threadbare.

5. "I must _____ that everyone take off their shoes," the librarian said in a loud voice.

6. Are you sure that the parakeet isn't just _____ the customers?

7. It is small _____ to the survivors that they will all be given a ride home.

Questions:

Indicate whether the following statements are True or False.

1. Rob was completely amazed when Beauchamp showed him the tiger.   T   or   F

2. Beauchamp referred to the tiger as "King of the jungle," however, it is usually a lion which is referred to as *king of the jungle*.   T   or   F

3. Beauchamp was considering the option of putting the tiger in front of the motel to draw customers.   T   or   F

4. Beauchamp gave Rob all the keys to the cage except the one for the main door.   T   or   F

5. Beauchamp told Rob that the tiger's name was Brutus.   T   or   F

6. When introducing Rob to the tiger, Beauchamp referred to Rob as the tiger's "meal ticket."   T   or   F

7. The tiger's stare reminded Rob of his mother's.   T   or   F

8. Rob was dismayed to see that Sistine was wearing his shirt and jeans when she got off the bus.   T   or   F

9. Two facts that Sistine researched about tigers were: panthers lived in the nearby woods and tigers are an endangered species.   T   or   F

10. Rob was amazed when Sistine began to cry at the end of Chapter 20.   T   or   F

The Tiger Rising
By Kate DiCamillo

Language Activities:

Find three examples of the following parts of speech from this chapter.

Nouns	Verbs	Ajectives

Extension Activity:

1. **Interview** at least three other students for their views of this novel thus far. (Try to get both positive and negative comments.) Write a brief **report** putting these views together.

    _____

    _____

    _____

    _____

    _____

    _____

2. We have already read about a number of important conflicts in this novel. **Conflict** is an important element in a novel. There are generally three types of conflict: **person against person; person against self; and person against nature**. Find three examples of conflict in The Tiger Rising and tell which type of conflict each is. (You don't have to get an example from each category.)

    a) _____

    _____

    _____

    b) _____

    _____

    _____

    c) _____

    _____

    _____

The Tiger Rising
By Kate DiCamillo

Chapters 21 & 22

Before you read the chapters:

Misunderstandings can be very upsetting to those involved. Describe a time in your life (or that of a friend) when a misunderstanding made your friendship with someone a little tense. How did it work out in the end?

_____

_____

_____

_____

Vocabulary:

Analogies are equations in which the first pair of words has the same relationship as the second pair of words. For example, **stop** is to **go** as **fast** is to **slow**. In this example, both pairs of words are opposites. Choose the best word from the word box to complete each of the analogies below.

reproach	extend	sorrow	recline	concentrate
materialize	prophetess	original	applied	desperate

1. **Disappear** is to _____ as **walk** is to **run**.

2. **Reckless** is to _____ as **six** is to **half-dozen**.

3. **Withdraw** is to _____ as **angry** is to **elated**.

4. **Seer** is to _____ as **woman** is to **female**.

5. **Earliest** is to _____ as **calm** is to **placid**.

6. **Praise** is to _____ as **wake** is to **sleep**.

7. **Break** is to **mend** as **daydream** is to _____.

8. **Ointment** is to **salve** as **lean** is to _____.

9. **Poem** is to **verse** as **used** is to _____.

10. **Stubborn** is to **placid** as **contentment** is to _____.

The Tiger Rising
By Kate DiCamillo

Questions:

1. How did Willie May greet Rob and Sistine at the beginning of Chapter 21?

_____

_____

_____

2. Why do you think Rob "desperately wanted" Willie May and Sistine to like each other?

_____

_____

_____

3. a) How did Sistine define a "prophetess?"

_____

_____

_____

   b) Why did Sistine consider Willie May to be a prophetess?

_____

_____

_____

4. What mistake did Rob make regarding the meat that Beauchamp had given him?

_____

_____

_____

5. According to Rob, what was the "original green?"

_____

_____

_____

The Tiger Rising
By Kate DiCamillo

Language Activities:

An **idiom** is a literary device that says one thing, but means another (i.e., *you hit the nail on the head*). An example from Chapter 22 is *"but then he thought of Beauchamp and held his tongue."* Think of another example of an **idiom** and record it below.

_____

_____

Extension Activity:

For Sale!

Imagine that Beauchamp decides he is going to sell the tiger and he asks Rob to design a "For Sale" poster that Beauchamp will reproduce and send to a number of zoos in the area. Your task is to design a poster for this project. Your poster should include contact information (i.e., Beauchamp's name; the tiger can be seen at the Kentucky Star Motel in Lister). You should also include a colored picture of a tiger and any other information (i.e., a price) that you think would be helpful and relevant to potential buyers.

The Tiger Rising
By Kate DiCamillo

Chapters 23 & 24

Before you read the chapters:

If you were Rob, would you consider telling an adult about the caged tiger? If so, who might you tell? Why?

_____

_____

_____

_____

_____

Vocabulary:

Choose a word from the list to complete each definition:

clench	disapproval	shag	enormous
purposeful	soothe	demand	fierce

1. To calm or comfort is to _____.

2. Someone who is _____ has an aim in mind.

3. To ask for something in a forceful manner is to make a _____.

4. To _____ means to grasp with your hand.

5. _____ means "menacingly wild" or "savage."

6. _____ entails a condemnatory feeling, look or utterance.

7. If a person is _____, then they are very large in size.

8. A _____ is a kind of rug.

The Tiger Rising
By Kate DiCamillo

Questions:

1. Why does Willie May ask Rob, "What you giving me them shifty-eyed looks for?"

   _____

   _____

2. Later in Chapter 23, Willie May says, "I ain't got to do nothing except stay black and die." What do you think this statement says about her state of mind and impression of herself?

   _____

   _____

   _____

3. What benefit did Rob think Willie May might enjoy now that she had the carving of the bird?

   _____

   _____

   _____

4. In Chapter 24, Rob comes to realize why he likes Sistine so much. What is this reason?

   _____

   _____

5. Why was Willie May wise not to give a direct answer to Sistine's question about whether she would release a captive animal?

   _____

   _____

6. Do you think that Willie May believes Rob and Sistine when she tells them to show her the tiger? Support your answer.

   _____

   _____

The Tiger Rising
By Kate DiCamillo

Language Activities:

Onomatopoeia is a literary device where sounds are spelled out as a word or when words describing sounds actually sound like the sounds they describe. An example from this chapter is *oof* (the sound of getting punched in the stomach). Think of examples of this literary device for the following:

Description	Onomatopoeia
the sound of someone stepping on a grape	
the sound of lightning on a dark night	
Your example:	
Your example:	

Antonyms, Synonyms or Homonyms

Beside each pair of words write **A** (antonym) or **S** (synonym) or **H** (homonym).

1. close - clothes   _____
2. open - close   _____
3. die - dye   _____
4. always - forever   _____
5. knew - new   _____
6. children - adults   _____
7. eye - I   _____
8. real - pretend   _____
9. real - reel   _____
10. two - too   _____

Storyboard

A storyboard is a series of pictures that tell the main events of a story. A storyboard can tell the story of only one scene – or the entire novel.

Complete the storyboard below illustrating your favorite scene from The Tiger Rising thus far.
You may wish to practice your drawings on a separate piece of paper.

1	2
3	**4**
5	**6**

The Tiger Rising
By Kate DiCamillo

Chapters 25 & 26

Before you read the chapters:

In Chapter 25, Willie May makes the comment, "Sometimes right don't count." Do you feel that Willie May is right? Defend your response.

_____

_____

_____

_____

Vocabulary:

Replace the words that are underlined in the sentences below with a word from the word list in the box. Remember to consider the context of the word in the sentences, as some words may have several meanings.

squint	horizon	exist	disgusted
cautioning	miraculous	sissy	conjure

1. Chad was **repulsed** by his cousin's behavior.   _____

2. Everyone in the class thought that Rob was a **wimp**.   _____

3. Her recovery from the disease was nothing short of **astonishing**.   _____

4. His **future** was regarded by everyone as quite bleak.   _____

5. Does Sistine **squinch** her eyes when she is deep in thought?   _____

6. The old woman thought she could **invoke** the wrath of the gods.   _____

7. His mother was **admonishing** him to be more careful when
   skateboarding.   _____

8. It would be almost impossible for anyone to **subsist** under
   such harsh circumstances.   _____

© On The Mark Press • S&S Learning Materials   48   OTM-14279 • SSN1-279 The Tiger Rising

The Tiger Rising
By Kate DiCamillo

Questions:

1. Willie May says, "One person in the world that don't need to be owning no tiger, and that's Beauchamp." What do you think there was about Beauchamp that gave her this opinion?

_____

_____

2. a) What was Willie May's reason for not releasing the tiger?

_____

_____

   b) What did Willie May say was the only thing that they could do for the tiger?

_____

_____

3. What caused Sistine to lash out at Rob and say such hurtful things to him?

_____

_____

4. How was Rob's plan to release the tiger in Chapter 26 interrupted?

_____

_____

5. Sistine makes the statement that she feels Beauchamp is afraid of the tiger. What clue do we have in Chapter 19 that she may be right?

_____

_____

6. We find the first reference to the title of this novel in Chapter 25 when Willie May says, "I would love to see this tiger rise up out of this cage." Perhaps the title is an example of **foreshadowing**. If so, how might the tiger "rise up" out of its cage?

_____

_____

The Tiger Rising
By Kate DiCamillo

Language Activities:

Try to reassemble the word parts listed below into eight compound words found in these chapters.

no	tooth	your	some	friend	with	way	side
in	body	self	pick	girl	high	out	times

1. _____

2. _____

3. _____

4. _____

5. _____

6. _____

7. _____

8. _____

Extension Activity:

Both Chapters, 25 and 26 end in exciting **cliffhanger** situations. Predict what you think will happen next in Chapter 27.

_____

_____

_____

_____

_____

_____

_____

_____

The Tiger Rising
By Kate DiCamillo

Comparing Two Characters

It is difficult to imagine two characters who could be more different than Rob and Sistine. In some ways they are quite similar, but mostly they are very different people (in appearance as well as temperament). **Compare** six things about these two people. Please try for a variety of criteria (i.e., physical appearance, personality, age, talents, attitude, etc.)

Criteria	Rob	Sistine
1.		
2.		
3.		
4.		
5.		
6.		

The Tiger Rising
By Kate DiCamillo

Chapters 27 & 28

Before you read the chapters:

Rita Mae Brown once wrote: "A peacefulness follows any decision, even the wrong one." The next chapter describes a decision made by Rob and its consequences. Some decisions turn out well and other have unpleasant results. Describe an important decision you once made, as well as its results. Did a feeling of peacefulness follow the decision?

_____

_____

_____

_____

Vocabulary:

Choose a word from the list to complete each sentence.

crouched	ignore	delicacy	furious
emancipate	oblivious	contained	gratitude

1. Rob made up his mind to _____ the tiger.

2. "That is a fine way to show your _____ after all I've done for you," his aunt said.

3. There is no doubt that the people of Kensington Market will be _____ if the huge apartment building is built by their only park.

4. My grandfather was _____ to the sound of traffic outside his home.

5. It is best to _____ insults whenever you can.

6. Oysters are considered to be a _____ in my hometown.

7. Sistine kept her emotions _____ within herself.

8. The huge tiger was _____ beneath a large eucalyptus tree.

The Tiger Rising
By Kate DiCamillo

Questions:

1. What was the tiger's initial response when Rob first opened the door to its cage?

   _____

   _____

   _____

2. What did Rob and Sistine have to do to make the tiger leave the cage?

   _____

   _____

   _____

3. Why do you think the tiger didn't attack Rob and Sistine when let out of the cage?

   _____

   _____

   _____

4. From the beginning of Chapter 28, prove that both Sistine and Rob had doubts about whether they did the right thing in letting the tiger go?

   _____

   _____

   _____

5. a) What resulted when Rob "opened the suitcase?"

   _____

   _____

   _____

   b) Do you think this was a good or bad thing for Rob? Why?

   _____

   _____

   _____

The Tiger Rising

By Kate DiCamillo

Extension Activity:

Create a **book cover** for *The Tiger Rising*. Be sure to include the title, author, and a picture that will make other students want to read the novel.

The Tiger Rising

By Kate DiCamillo

Chapters 29 & 30

Before you read the chapters:

As you begin the final chapters, describe what you think would be the perfect ending to this novel.

_____

_____

_____

_____

Vocabulary:

Draw a straight line to connect the vocabulary word to its definition. Remember to use a straight edge (like a ruler).

1.	recite	a.	harmony
2.	immortal	b.	wonder
3.	aspire	c.	eternal
4.	symmetry	d.	contemplate
5.	experience	e.	sensible
6.	marvel	f.	repeat
7.	reasonable	g.	confess
8.	concentrate	h.	engrossed
9.	consider	i.	encounter
10.	admit	j.	want

The Tiger Rising
By Kate DiCamillo

1. What contribution did Sistine make to the funeral ceremony for the tiger? Do you think this was appropriate? Explain your answer.

_____

_____

2. Do you think it was appropriate that Willie May gave the carving of the bird to the tiger in its burial, seeing that Rob had given this to her as a gift?

_____

_____

3. Sistine apologizes to Rob on two occasions in Chapter 29. What were the two things she apologized for?

_____

_____

4. What was Rob's dad going to make Rob do to make him face the consequence of his actions? What consequence might Rob's dad still face?

_____

_____

5. Why do you think it was so necessary for Rob to hear his mother's name?

_____

_____

6. The climax of a story occurs when the main problem of the story is solved. When does the climax of the novel occur?

_____

_____

7. Describe your feelings about this novel. What was one thing you really enjoyed, and one thing you think that the author might have improved upon?

_____

_____

The Tiger Rising
By Kate DiCamillo

Extension Activity:

Story Map

Complete the following Story Map from the reading of *The Tiger Rising*.

Setting: Approximate Time: Place:

Characters: Major: Minor:

Problem/Challenge:

Plot/Events: (At least six items)

Resolution (Climax):

Answer Key

Chapters 1 - 2 *(Page 10)*

Vocabulary:

1. harbors 2. notion 3. abiding 4. astounded 5. sullen
6. lurch 7. concentrating 8. creeping 9. melody 10. pretend

Questions:

1. He thought it might bring him luck.
2. He would rather be eaten by a bear than go to school.
3. *Answers will vary.*
4. The rash on his legs; his mother; getting onto the bus.
5. He imagined stuffing all his feelings in a suitcase and locking it shut.
6. Present day Lister, Florida.
7. Answers will vary. (i.e., <u>Verbal</u>: "You ain't a star nowhere." <u>Physical</u>: Billy grabbed Rob's hair, ground his knuckles into Rob's scalp.)
8. A new girl got on the bus.

Chapters 3 - 4 *(Page 13)*

Vocabulary:

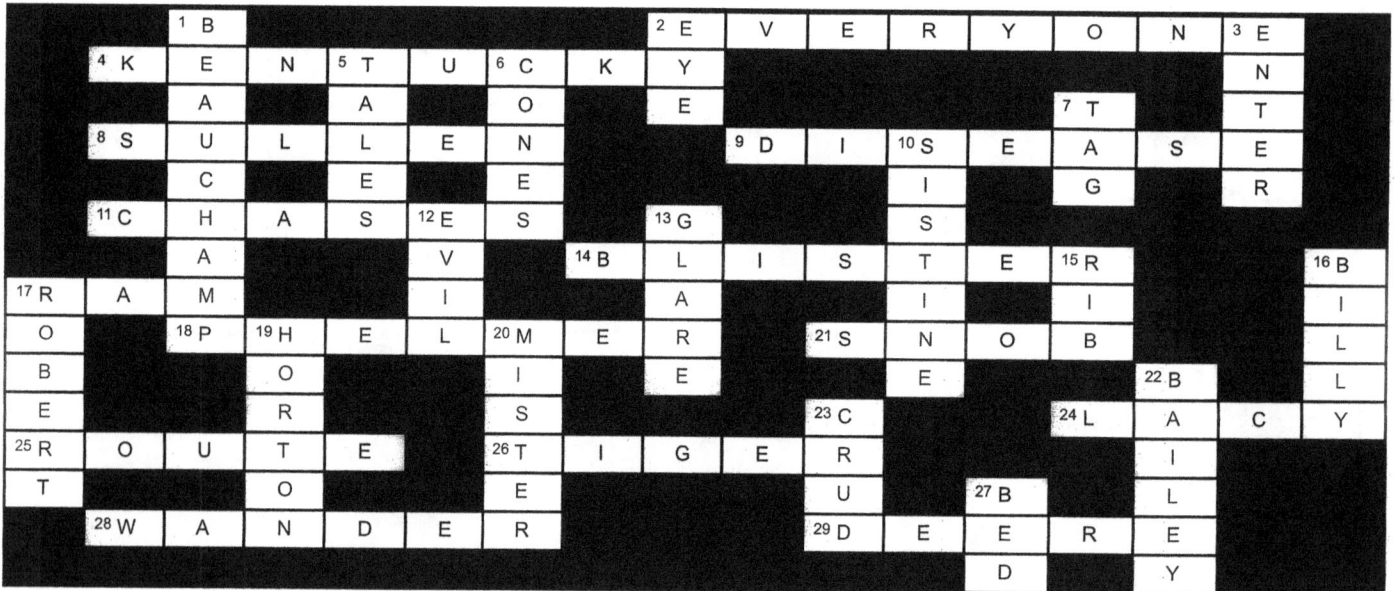

Questions:

1. Rob had a rash on his legs.
2. Sistine was wearing a "party" dress.
3. *Answers will vary.* (i.e., she had a sharp nose, sharp chin and black eyes; she spoke distinctly; she wasn't intimidated by Billy and Norton).
4. He didn't think of troublesome things.
5. Philadelphia. She hates the south because the people are ignorant.
6. *Answers will vary.* (i.e., It is Jason that trips him – so we know that it isn't just Billy and Norton who pick on him.)

Language Activities:

1. <u>C</u>ookie <u>c</u>utter.

Chapter 5 - 6 *(Page 16)*

Vocabulary:

1. council   2. selfish   3. manifest   4. sabotaged   5. possibility   6. vestibule   7. fortitude

Questions:

Mr. Phelmer always began his talks with Rob by saying, "Rob, we're a bit <u>worried</u>. The fact that Rob didn't <u>interact</u> with other students was a concern. Mr. Phelmer asked Rob if he was putting medicine on his <u>legs</u>. Some parents were worried that Rob's rash might be <u>contagious</u>. A <u>doctor</u> in Jacksonville gave Rob the medicine. Mr. Phelmer suggested that Rob stay at <u>home</u> until his rash cleared up. Rob thought that was a <u>great</u> idea. When visiting the principal, Rob felt the picture of the <u>tiger</u> burning in his pocket. After his visit with Mr. Phelmer was over, the principal gave him a <u>note</u> to take home. Rob knew that his legs would <u>never</u> clear up.

At lunch, Rob sat on the benches in the <u>breezeway</u>. Nothing had tasted good to him since his <u>mother</u> died. Sistine Bailey then came through the <u>lunchroom</u> doors followed by a crowd of <u>kids</u>. When someone threw <u>something</u> at Sistine she turned and started swinging with her fists, <u>kicking</u> and twirling. When Rob told the kids to leave her alone, they <u>looked</u> at him. After a minute Rob decided to <u>run</u>.

Chapters 7 - 8 *(Page 19)*

Vocabulary:

1. (e)   2. (h)   3. (a)   4. (j)   5. (b)   6. (i)   7. (c)   8 (d)   9. (f)   10. (g)

Questions:

1. *Answers will vary.* (i.e., Been bullied on the bus and at school; met Sistine; been to the principal's office; excused from school; saw a tiger in the woods.)
2. *Answers will vary.* (i.e., prevented him from further hurt.)
3. *Answers will vary.* (i.e., until he gets a better job or saves up some money.)
4. He knew that Rob was being bullied by the other students.
5. *Answers will vary.*
6. *Answers will vary.* (i.e., perhaps he thought he had imagined the tiger and he would be disappointed.)
7. Sistine had made an impression on him.

Language Activities:

bodies; men; roofs; people; macaroni; dresses; ointments; feet

Chapters 9 - 10 *(Page 22)*

Vocabulary:

1. personal   2. extended   3. desperate   4. adjust
5. licorice   6. capable   7. certificates   8. rhythm

Questions:

1. He was afraid if he started wishing, he might not be able to stop.
2. *Answers will vary.* (i.e., Rob's dad says, "If it don't stop soon, the whole state ain't going to be nothing but a big swamp."
3. *Answers will vary.* (i.e., wispy.)
4. It brought back memories of his late wife.
5. Willie Mays.
6. Without an education, he would not get a good job.
7. "You keeping all that sadness down low, in your legs. You not letting it get up to your heart, where it belongs." *Answers will vary.*

Language Activities:

Alphabetical Order: shyly; smashing; softly; squeak; star; stared; steam; stop; suitcase; swamp

Chapters 11 - 12 *(Page 25)*

Vocabulary:

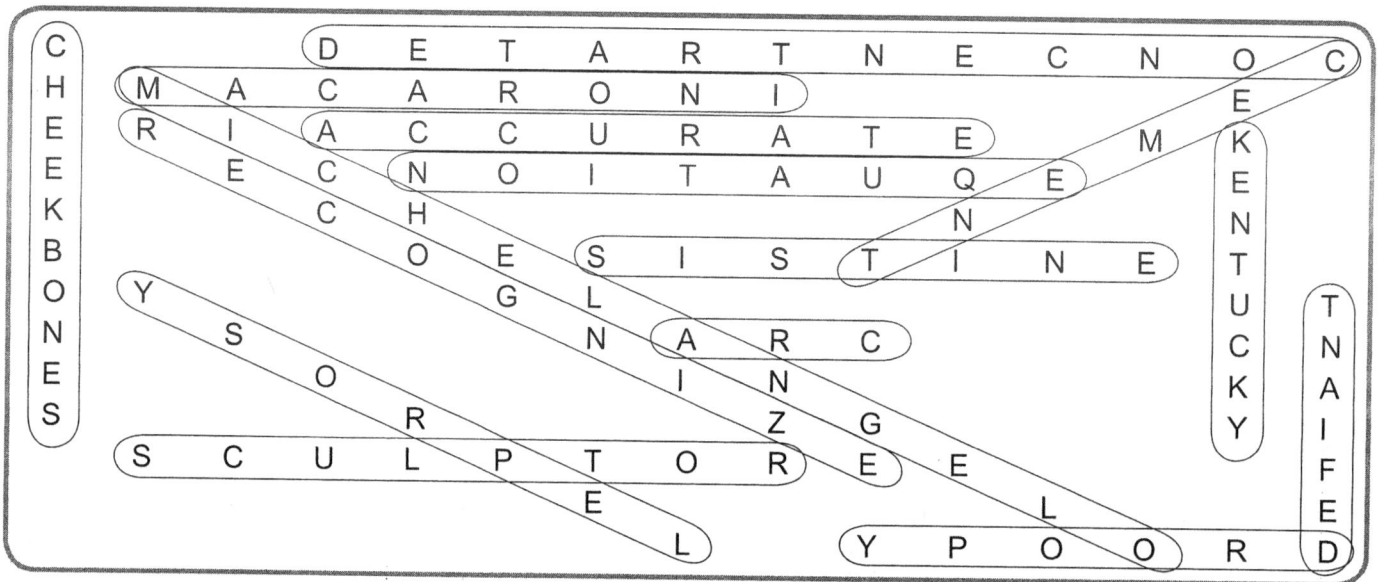

Questions:

1. Leprosy.
2. *Answers will vary.* (i.e., to keep from being hurt.)
3. *Answers will vary.*
4. She was impressed.
5. It is caused by stress.
6. *Answers will vary.*

Language Activities:

Rob and **S**istine lived in the town of **L**ister.
Why do you think **P**rincipal **P**helmer was worried about **R**ob?
This August, we will be visiting **B**oston, **P**ittsburgh and **T**oronto on our vacation.

Chapters 13 - 14 *(Page 29)*

Vocabulary:

Answers will vary.

Questions:

1. Her parents split up so her mother moved back to Lister, where she grew up.
2. "Rob felt a familiar loneliness rise up and drape its arms over his shoulder."
3. a) Speaking of her caused him pain.
   b) She had shared personal things about herself to Rob.
4. He was enormous and bright.
5. Let the tiger go free.
6. "The feeling that was pushing up inside him, filling him full to overflowing."

Chapters 15 - 16 *(Page 31)*

Vocabulary:

1. squint	2. constellation	3. evaporate	4. grease	5. concentrate
6. stalk	7. congressman	8. forbidden	9. disbelief	10. profile

Questions:

1. She can't wait to move away from Lister.
2. She says, "Good grief. Well, can I have some change at least?"
3. Rob was upset that he had displayed feeling, for it made the world seem a sadder place.
4. They were in the Sistine Chapel looking up at the ceiling and bumped into each other.
5. Everyone in Jacksonville wanted to talk to Rob's dad about his dead wife, and he couldn't bear it.
6. a) *Answers will vary.*
   b) *Answers will vary.* (i.e., they had different ideas about the way Sistine should act, dress, etc.)

Chapters 17 - 18 *(Page 34)*

Vocabulary:

1. (b) 2. (d) 3. (a) 4. (b) 5. (c) 6. (a) 7. (d)

Questions:

1. a) *Answers will vary.* (i.e., to get an adult's opinion).
   b) *Answers will vary.*
2. *Answers will vary.* (i.e., he was loud, braggart, bully, coward).
3. *Answers will vary.* (i.e., he wanted to see the tiger but didn't want Beauchamp to be a part of it).
4. *Answers will vary.* (i.e., he pays him to feed the tiger).

Language Activities:

1. *Answers will vary.*
2. a) fold b) nod c) final d) go

Chapters 19 - 20 *(Page 38)*

Vocabulary:

insist - suggest; tattered - new; desperate – hopeful; amazing - ordinary; mocking - sincere; comfort - uneasiness; whisper - shout.

1. whisper 2. amazing 3. desperate 4. tattered 5. insist 6. mocking 7. comfort

Questions:

1. False 2. True 3. True 4. False 5. False 6. True 7. False 8.True 9. True 10. True

Chapters 21 - 22 *(Page 41)*

Vocabulary:

1. materialize   2. desperate   3. extend   4. prophetess   5. original
6. reproach   7. concentrate   8. recline   9. applied   10. sorrow

Questions:

1. She said "boo" to them.
2. *Answers will vary.* (i.e., an increased sense of security for himself.)
3. a) Women who God speaks through.
   b. *Answers will vary.* (i.e., Willie May was very insightful and wise.)
4. He left the meat where his dad was able to find it.
5. The first one God ever thought up.

Chapters 23 - 24 *(Page 44)*

Vocabulary:

1. soothe   2. purposeful   3. demand   4. clench   5. fierce   6. disapproval   7. enormous   8. shag

Questions:

1. Rob wanted to give her the carving of the bird and he was working up the nerve.
2. *Answers will vary.*
3. She wouldn't dream of her pet bird anymore.
4. He liked her because when she saw something beautiful, the sound of her voice changed.
5. *Answers will vary.* (It is always wise to get all the facts before answering such a question.)
6. *Answers will vary.*

Language Activities:

1. Homonyms   2. Antonyms   3. Homonyms   4. Synonyms   5. Homonyms
6. Antonyms   7. Homonyms   8. Antonyms   9. Homonyms   10. Homonyms

Chapters 25 - 26 *(Page 48)*

Vocabulary:

1. disgusted   2. sissy   3. miraculous   4. horizon   5. squint   6. conjure   7. cautioning   8. exist

Questions:

1. *Answers will vary.* (i.e., She didn't think he was responsible enough to be looking after a tiger.)
2. a) How's it going to live?
   b) Let it be.
3. Rob told Sistine that her dad wasn't coming for her and that her dad was a liar.
4. Beauchamp arrived on the scene.
5. He was obviously frightened when feeding the tiger as he jumped back and was sweating profusely.
6. *Answers will vary.* (i.e., perhaps it would escape, be released or die.)

Language Activities:

Possible Compound Words: nobody; yourself; sometimes; highway; inside; toothpick; girlfriend; without

Chapters 27 - 28 *(Page 52)*

Vocabulary:

1. emancipate   2. gratitude   3. furious   4. oblivious   5. ignore   6. delicacy   7. contained   8. crouched

Questions:

1. It ignored Rob and the open door.
2. They shook the cage and screamed at the tiger.
3. *Answers will vary.* (i.e., it wasn't hungry; it was distracted by freedom)
4. Sistine says "that was the right thing to do" twice, as if convincing herself. Rob remembers what happened to Cricket, Willie May's bird.
5. a) The words sprang out of it, coiled and explosive.
   b) Good. It released all the pent-up emotion and feelings he had been harboring since his mother's death.

Chapters 29 - 30 *(Page 55)*

Vocabulary:

1. f 2. c 3. j 4. a 5. i 6. b 7. e 8. h 9. d 10. g

Questions:

1. She quoted a verse from the poem "The Tiger" by William Blake.
2. *Answers will vary.*
3. For making him release the tiger and for the cruel things she said to him.
4. Admit to Beauchamp that he released the tiger. Rob's dad might lose his job at the motel.
5. *Answers will vary.* (i.e., so Rob would have a way of expressing his feelings about his mother and not having them locked inside.)
6. *Answers will vary.* (i.e., when the tiger is released/shot and Rob releases his pent-up emotions to his dad)
7. *Answers will vary.*

Story Map *(Page 57)*

Setting:
Lister, Florida, Present day.

Characters:
Major: Rob, Sistine.
Minor: Willie May, Rob's dad, Sistine's mom, Beauchamp.

Problem:
Rob has locked away all of his sorrow and grief regarding his mother's recent death. He needs a way of releashing these pent-up emotions so as to begin the healing process.

Plot:
Answers will vary. Rob finds a caged tiger near his home and meets a new friend, Sistine. They decide to release the tiger, which Rob's father shoots. Rob is grief-stricken as a result and vents his feelings on his father, releasing all the pent-up sorrow he has been storing inside himself.

Resolution:
Now that his grief has been released, Rob is able to come to terms with losing his mother and is able to move on with his life, establishing a healthy friendship with Sistine.

THE CRICKET IN TIMES SQUARE

by George Selden

List of Skills

Vocabulary Development

1. Using content clues
2. Locating descriptive words/phrases
3. Listing synonyms, antonyms, homonyms
4. Use of capitals and punctuation
5. Identifying syllables
6. Listing compound words
7. Determining alphabetical order
8. Use of singular/plural nouns
9. Developing dictionary skills
10. Identifying parts of speech
11. Identify an *analogy*
12. Identifying an *idiom*
13. Identifying a *simile*
14. Identify *alliteration*.

Setting Activities

1. Identify the details of a setting

Plot Activities

1. Complete a Story Map
2. Identify *conflict* in the story
3. Determine the role of others in one's personal growth
4. Develop a Storyboard
5. Identify a *cliffhanger*
6. Identify the *climax* of a novel
7. Develop a synopsis.

Character Activities

1. Determine character traits
2. Compare two characters
3. Relating personal experiences
4. Understand concepts: *friendship, perseverance*

Creative and Critical Thinking

1. Research
2. Complete 5 W's Chart
3. Write a letter to a friend
4. Conduct an interview
5. Create a KWL Chart
6. Write a description of personal feelings

Art Activities

1. Design a cricket house
2. Design a cover for the novel
3. Develop a Storyboard

THE CRICKET IN TIMES SQUARE

by George Selden

Teacher Suggestions

This resource can be used in a variety of ways:

1. The student booklet focuses on one chapter of the novel at a time. Each of these sections contains the following activities:

   a) **Before you read the chapters** (reasoning and critical thinking skills)
   b) **Vocabulary building** (dictionary and thesaurus skills)
   c) **Questions on the chapter** (reading comprehension skills)
   d) **Language activities** (grammar, punctuation, word structure, and extension activities)

2. Students may read the novel at their own speed and then select, or be assigned, a variety of questions and activities.

3. **Bulletin Board and Interest Center Ideas:** Themes might include crickets; New York City; Times Square; subways and subway stations; Italian opera; mice; cats; Chinese culture.

4. **Pre-Reading Activities:** The Cricket in Times Square may also be used in conjunction with themes of animals in literature; music/opera; friendship; relocating to new places; facing adversity; developing personal responsibility; doing the thoughtful/honorable thing.

5. **Independent Reading Approach:** Students who are able to work independently may attempt to complete the assignments in a self-directed manner. Initially these students should participate in the pre-reading activities with the rest of the class. Students should familiarize themselves with the reproducible student booklet. Completed worksheets should be submitted so that the teacher can note how quickly and accurately the students are working. Students may be brought together periodically to discuss issues in specific sections of the novel.

6. **Fine Art Activities**: Students may integrate such topics as greeting cards, abstract art, costumes, and posters.

7. Encourage the students to keep a reading log in which they record their readings each day and their thoughts about the passage.

8. Students should keep all their work together in one place. A portfolio cover is provided for this reason.

9. Students should not be expected to complete all activities. Teachers should allow choice and in some cases, match the activity to the student's ability.

10. Students should keep track (in their portfolio) of the activities they complete.

THE CRICKET IN TIMES SQUARE

by George Selden

Synopsis

The Cricket in Times Square is the story of Chester Cricket and his unexpected journey from the countryside of Connecticut to a subway station in Times Square, New York City. There he meets Tucker Mouse and Harry Cat who befriend him and teach him how to survive in this unfamiliar and frightening environment. Chester is also befriended by a young boy, Mario, whose parents own the newsstand in which Chester has taken shelter.

Chester does not get off to the best of starts in his new home: he eats a two dollar bill belonging to Mario's family, and then he and his animal friends almost burn the newsstand to the ground. It is only when it is discovered that Chester has an amazing musical talent that things begin to turn around for the cricket and his friends.

Chester learns a number of musical compositions by listening to the radio in the evenings, and he begins to give concerts to the people in the subway station, attracting great crowds and improving business for Mario's family. But despite his newfound fame, Chester is not happy. He longs for his home in Connecticut. Finally, he lets Mario know that he is leaving and with the help of Tucker and Harry, he catches the train back to Connecticut.

The Cricket in Times Square is a wonderful story which emphasizes the importance of friendship and doing the honorable thing, no matter the consequence, and looking out for the feelings of others.

Author Biography

George Selden was the pen name of George Selden Thompson, who was born in the same state as Chester the Cricket, Connecticut. Although George wrote over fifteen books and two plays, **The Cricket in Times Square** was his most famous. He explained the inspiration for that book as follows:

> *"One night I was coming home on the subway, and I did hear a cricket chirp in the Times Square subway station. The story formed in my mind within minutes."*

A number of novels featuring Chester, Tucker and Harry followed, including: **Tucker's Countryside, Harry Cat's Pet Puppy**, and **Chester Cricket's Pigeon Ride**.

Mr. Selden lived in New York City until his death in December 1989. He enjoyed music, archaeology, and J.R.R. Tolkien.

THE CRICKET IN TIMES SQUARE

by George Selden

Student Checklist

Student Name: _____

Assignment	Grade/Level	Comments

THE CRICKET IN TIMES SQUARE

by George Selden

NEWSPAPERS

Daily Times

Daily Times
The Cricket in Times Square!

Subway
Times Square
42 Street Station
A C E N Q R W
S 1 2 3 7

Name: _____

THE CRICKET IN TIMES SQUARE

by George Selden

Before you read the chapter:

Chapter 1

Times Square is a major intersection in New York City and is considered to be a symbol of the city. Investigate this famous landmark and record <u>three</u> interesting facts about it.

_____

_____

_____

_____

Think of at least one <u>advantage</u> and one <u>disadvantage</u> to working at a newsstand in a busy subway station.

_____

_____

_____

Vocabulary:

Choose a word from the list to complete each sentence.

grilles	pity	subsided	vanished	abandoned
niche	shuttle	scrounge	displayed	gust

1. Tucker liked to _____ bits of paper and shreds of cloth.

2. The old mansion had been _____ for as long as anyone could remember.

3. By midnight, the traffic in the subway station had _____ somewhat.

www.ingramcontent.com/pod-product-compliance
Lightning Source LLC
Chambersburg PA
CBHW080524090426
42734CB00015B/3148